SING A NEW SONG

A Book of Psalms

BIJOU LE TORD

William B. Eerdmans Publishing Company
Grand Rapids, Michigan   Cambridge, U.K.

© 1997 Wm. B. Eerdmans Publishing Co.

255 Jefferson Ave. S.E., Grand Rapids, Michigan 49503

P. 0. Box 163, Cambridge CB3 9PU U.K.

01 00 99 98 97   7 6 5 4 3 2 1

Library of Congress Cataloging-in-Publication Data

Bible. O.T. Psalms. English. Le Tord. Selections. 1997.

Sing a new song : a book of Psalms / [compiled] by Bijou Le Tord.

L.C.

Summary: Watercolor illustrations accompany these retellings of

psalms arranged for daily reading.

ISBN 0-8028-5139-8 (cloth : alk. paper)

1.Bible. O.T. Psalms - juvenile literature.

2. Children - Prayer books and devotions - English.

[1. Bible. O.T. Psalms. 2. Prayer books and devotions.]

1. Le Tord, Bijou.   11. Title.

BS1423.L47 1997

223'.209505 - dc2O   96-33231

CIP

ISBN 0-8028-5139-8

Book design by Joy Chu

Printed in Hong Kong by South China Printing Co. (1988) ltd.

For Scott and Megan,
Rowenna, Liam and Levin,
with love

The Lord is like a sun,

shining on the universe.

Psalm 85:11

Let the earth

be happy.

Psalm 97:1

Let all the islands sing,

Psalm 97:1

and the mountains bring peace.

Psalm 72:3

You visited the earth,

and watered it.

Psalm 65:9

You blessed the little seeds,

springing above the soil.

Psalm 65:10

You made snow

like wool.

Psalm 147:16

You fly

the wings of the wind.

Psalm 18:10

No one

knows your footprints.

Psalm 77:19

You are

the silver wings of the dove.

Psalm 68:13

Oh, that I had wings

like a dove!

Psalm 55:6

I will sing a new song,

to You, dear Lord.

Psalm 96:1

I will praise You with all my heart,

Psalm 9:1

play my trumpet in the new moon.

Psalm 81:3

And the fields will also sing

in happiness.

Psalm 65:13

And Lord, You said:
"I will guide you with my eyes."

Psalm 32:8

For You are my hiding place.

Psalm 32:7

And Your Love is like a great mountain.

Psalm 36:6